Goodbye, Silver Sister

Goodbye, Silver Sister

POEMS

Jeanne Foster

TriQuarterly Books/Northwestern University Press
Evanston, Illinois

TriQuarterly Books
Northwestern University Press
www.nupress.northwestern.edu

Printed in the United States of America

10   9   8   7   6   5   4   3   2   1

Library of Congress Cataloging-in-Publication Data
Foster, Jeanne, 1941– author.
 Goodbye, silver sister : poems / Jeanne Foster.
  pages cm
 ISBN 978-0-8101-3128-6 (pbk. : alk. paper) — ISBN 978-0-8101-3129-3 (ebook)
 I. Title.
 PS3606.O754G66 2015
 811.6—dc23

                    2015005980

With love for my parents
Buford Alexandra Mecklin Foster
Charles Clarence Foster

CONTENTS

in gratitude

Goodbye, Silver Sister

One

Listening to a Shell

The tongue is tough. It doesn't want to let go.
In the remnant light, my sandy-haired uncle
grasps it with pliers. He is gilded bronze
in his bathing suit. The tongue is pink as salmon,
the color of the last sky. The harder he pulls,
the deeper it draws back into labyrinthine whorls.
He sets a screwdriver like a chisel
against the center point, the temple
where the tapering spiral peaks, perfection
that speaks of something larger.
And now he taps the handle with a hammer,
a single well-placed blow, and the tip of shell
flies off, lost in the sand. It's easy now.
The tongue surrenders, shuddering
its full length arrested from its house.
Gathered round, we witness Uncle Max
flay the naked animal, using true sand
for sandpaper. Then he rinses it
in the ocean's lapping edge. *The skin is tough,*
the raw tongue is crispy like cucumber,
he says, slicing each one of us a chunk
palpably shrinking in the hand.
There in the twilight I eat my one bite
of living conch. Only a shadow now
and a circular glow of cigarette,
my mother who knows secret things
cups the empty conch shell
to my ear. *Listen.*
Her breath swirls against my cheek.
Can you hear it?

The Bed Table Drawer

In there were her underwear, glowing
in their own lunar light, her panties
folded twice and tucked under themselves,
nested like silvery mushrooms in the arm of night.
Reaching into her things made my skin crawl
and my teeth hurt. Holding them up,
they were big, bigger than I thought.
Some stretched at the waist, some loose
in the legs. I imagined them at Woolworth's
under her skirts, or at the stove
when she cooked, or in the car
on the way to school. I saw them
once on the floor beside the bed
next to his. I tried on her shoes,
her dresses, her hats, but her panties,
I refolded and put back. Something in me
forbade I try on that shape
of things to come.

The Pianist

I lay against that sloping body,
feminine in its layers, a voice
more felt than heard, vibrating
like the pipes of an organ
through the crater of his chest to my ear
pressed against the folds,
stripes parading like majorettes
down his shirt, my cheek
a leaf riding the explosions
of his laughter. Something
like steam came off him.
Chubby fingers, dimpled wrists,

at the concert piano, tails hanging,
heavy legs working the pedals,
head raised in a showy ecstasy,
the lip, the nose, everything reared back,
a baby elephant on his haunches,
trunk furled, his hands commanded the keys.
In the backseat of my parents' Dodge, while he
entertained the two of them in the front seat
with his Hungarian burlesque of the American taste
for "hamburgers and Coca-Cola music," by which he meant
a woman's buttocks and Tchaikovsky's works,

he toyed with my breasts, and they
chose not to see. My father
traded, I think, blindness
for a performance of his piano *Sonatina*,
and my mother under the guise of decorum
fed her hunger for things foreign. I abhorred

his tyrannosaurus friend, the French zoologist,
tiny head perched atop a lizard body that listed
like the tower at Pisa, and managed to escape
his slurping affections in the front room at Thanksgiving
by slithering through the truncated limbs
down the reptilian skin and out between the gouty legs,
my blouse riding up to my chin, but the pianist,

I don't know why I loved that elephantine shape,
and snuggled, a leggy nymph,
deeper into his womanly heat, the fine spray
of saliva misting down on me
as he over-enunciated everything.

Fencing

You had to hold your head
just right to slip the mask
over the top, the padded brace along the back
curved to fit the skull. I loved the smell
of metal mixed with sweat and oil.
I loved looking through the tiny squares
of hard black screen, mounded like a featureless face,
toward that other dancing bird
who also had outgrown his cage,
and hearing his voice come back
steady with instruction. Already
we had put on the padded muslin
breastplate, over the head,
tied in back at the waist.
He taught me to hold the foil
between two fingers, fingers
facing upward, wrist flexible
and loose for parry and thrust. The left elbow
bent at right angle, hand up behind my head.
"Bend your knees," he said. He taught me
to lunge, aiming the capped tip
for the heart. Mostly he touched me.
The willowy foil tickled,
bending me double with laughter.
That was before I grew the chest
and jaw of death, divorce, and the thousand
other ways I would lose faith
in the breastplate of love.
If I could laugh again the way I laughed

when my father shouted, "Touché!"
and touched my heart,
bent double with the sobs,
I could stand again
in a body of love.

Painting a Still Life with My Mother

We painted at the dining room table,
each with our own paper,
a parallel concentration.
And as the vase
was doubly re-created,
a current flowed between us
of presence, ease, and pleasure.

On paper the deep mauve bulb
of the vase in a wash of color
stretched its long neck,
the line between air and glass
almost lost at the hint of lip,
something like the way
the great blue wading bird
we saw yesterday at Tomales Bay
leaned into flight.

What I want to say, Mother,
is that certain moments take,
the way a vaccination or a permanent wave
or a dye or a campaign
or a seed or a root or a flame
or an idea takes,
in a child's heart.
They remind the child that she is safe.
They remind the child that she is good.

Bagdad, Florida

One of those terrifyingly sleepy
towns you never heard of, decaying
porches, junk heaps, the scent of sweet
weeds; bare-chested barefoot kids with a space between
the two front teeth, a lisp to their shrieks;
the Mission Light Baptist Church calling its devils
and its angels. My mother's tribe

pounded the earth—the six sisters,
Buford, Janie, Cora, Evelyn, Carrie, Pauline,
and their various husbands and their children
and the various cousins—beside the black bay. My mother

escaped, walking into a lot when she was eighteen—
she'd never driven a car before—she bought
a Model A and drove away, the only problem was
she didn't know how to back up. She drove
to art school on Peachtree Street

in Atlanta, Georgia. I think she found unspeakable
the common, awkward, terror of those lives,
unspeakable in the hearing of a child, and so I heard it mentioned
only once—overheard it mentioned—that Buster . . .

Buster, whom I met two, three times—he was Pauline's husband,
maybe Carrie's—in his worn undershirt, khaki pants,
with cigar, a shriveled man, who didn't talk much. In fact,
I can't remember ever hearing him utter a word,
although he must have said hello

and goodbye. He mostly went outside
to get away. So did I.

He took us out once in the flat-bottomed boat by night,
poling without a sound over the bay, mosquitoes,
lightning bugs, a lantern hung low on the bow just above
the surface. In the shallows the flatfish lay—one eye,
staring into the sand over centuries and finding nothing
important, having migrated to join the other on the upward side
in a miracle of adaptation—both eyes now startled
by the light. His spear, poised, came down, clean,
found its mark. Impaled, the blind silver underside
flashed for a moment against the sky, before he tossed
the flounder to the bottom of the boat. Without a word,
we poled on.

I overheard my mother tell my father that Buster . . .
Buster squatted under the train trestle
and died. In her voice there was a tone—
wondering and at the same time judging—as though
he were guilty of death or guilty in death. I think it meant
she could see herself in him and still felt shamed
that one of them had come to live like a wild animal
out in a hovel where the tracks start to cross the bay.
I don't know how he died.

A moccasin bite, pure grain alcohol, or just plain
giving up, the way one who has seen the bright underside
is ready to fall into the sleep of the town,
as overhead the train click clicks.

The Bridge

We are crossing the bridge like all bridges
grown narrower with the passage of time.
Fishermen along each side
press ribs against railings,
leaning
toward that underworld of water
which is the fish's home
or heaven.
Caught forever under their straw hats,
they are leaning against the sky.

I open my palm, grown smaller,
and the underworld of a woman
is discovered
in the backseat of the car,
skin sticking to plastic covers,
as my father looks over his shoulder.
I sing to my small self,
growing smaller, mile upon mile
behind heads.

I am Judy Garland
on the yellow brick road. I am Maria Tallchief
on toe. On this bridge
I am magic. I sing my song
and the world melts.
Past lean fishermen and their leaner poles,
past gulls sighing like the wind
around our closed car windows
into the night.

And always the hum of the tires,
and the reassuring drone of the front seat voices,
and the bridge straight in the headlights,
and the brackish brown voice of the lake
unhurried like southern speech,
and the breathing creatures
underneath.

We would go down,
I hear the fishermen intoning,
we would go down and join you
in your home, where
you are still in shadow
and move in wakes of silence,
where we can hear nothing,
nothing but our own hearts
beating, like the bubbles that flow upward
when your slow mouth opens.
We would go down.

Two

The Pearl River

This little finger, she reassured,
rolling the baseball-stunned knuckle
of the child's left little finger between her padded thumb
and forefinger, couldn't be broken.
It is so limber, it could be bent
like a sapling under weight of snow to earth
and not snap.

Fawn and doe
stop at the side of the road
and turn their heads.

She is as doe to fawn,
that teacher, who only once
became enraged and broke
the scissors against the desk. The little girl sat
amazed.

But fingers . . .
I've said what I could say
about them.

The knobby limbs of the fawn
look fragile, as if they might be broken
by the slightest misstep
in the stubble, as she whisks
into shadow.

We who have felt pain in the heart
like the stab of a broken rib, whisper to ourselves
and bend over the young sea horse

unfurling its head
from the heart of a fern.
And smell the rich earth at the floor of the woods.
And smell the sprouting of pubic hairs.

Baby, baby, baby,
you are nothing but a crystal skull
we hold up to the moonlight
for seeing what might have been,
a different life
paralleling this one,
as the equator runs around the
belly of the earth
and the tropic of concern
around its head.

For this child too has seen the head of hen
separated from
the body of hen,
for she too has seen the chunky
body of hen, separated from
the head of hen, run circles
around the tree stump, where hatchet and head lay,
run headless under the calm, observant gaze
of the loblolly pines.

And the house was watched over,
its silver-tin roof shooting light from the sun
into the very hearts of those pines.
The swing on the screened porch
never completely still, creaking gently,
was occupied by the breeze
or an aunt's prevision of the days
after her last days. And the clearing
around the house absorbed the fall

of footsteps, stored in the needle-covered memory bank
of soil.

Nothing was simply let go.

She in her blue pinafore, trimmed with tiny red and yellow
flowers and green leaves, was afraid
of the very cousins—the red-haired Jim
and the green-eyed Barbara and their hairy friend.
She on the card table under the sheet,
the toiling witches above her.
She didn't know what would happen.
But nothing was let go.

The late nights of canasta under the yellow lights,
the taste of the cigarette,
the tree house,
the rattler,
the artesian well,
the water moccasins,
the swimming hole.
Nothing would let go.
Their shouts went into the secret hearts of the pines
and were never let go.

For this child too has been awakened from sleep
by a thumping of wings
inside the pillow,
by shoes shuffling in the closet,
has arisen and entered the tunnel behind
the rack of clothes,
crept down the stairs
to the water's edge,
where the boat waits.
For this child too has inherited the oven.

The Pearl River, the dividing line,
winds like a water moccasin through the red clay soil.
The moon turns its full face toward
the upward turned face, and the river shines
like pearl. Upon its surface
a water moccasin carves the shape
of a worker's scythe. A shadow
white as a madonna lily moves from the shore
into the pines. Everything was kept
under their cloaks. The song
curls like smoke back into the carapace
of a white girl's ear.

Kept all these years,
a treasure watched over by the pirate's ghost,
the pearl in the oyster growing in a bed of mud,
the milk before it is milked from the fangs,

the song wants a whiff of the heavy incense of its forefathers,
the southern pines, to unfold itself, it wants
the mockingbird's notes, to recall itself
from the labyrinth.

A water moccasin going home
on the surface of the Pearl River carves
the scythes of negro workers. A black man
at the water's edge raises his voice
to the moon who learned long ago to turn
its full face toward the upward turned face
shining like black silver. A shadow
white as a madonna lily moves away
under the dark green cloaks of our forefathers,
the loblolly pines. A slender woman walks out the other side
into daylight.

For she too has seen the hen
run in circles around the tree stump,
the foreshortened life running out
of the headless body like the breath
from a nightmaring mouth.

Baby, baby, baby,
you are nothing but a crystal skull
we hold up to the moonlight
for seeing what might have been.

The swing on the screened porch
occupied by the breeze or an aunt's prevision
of the days after her last
days.

Everything is kept, but nothing
is easily recovered.

Uncle Al laid down the hatchet.
The green-eyed Barbara, the red-haired Jim,
and Harry, their friend, stood around and watched.
The parents watched.
Those sober pines stood around
and watched.
Young things are so fragile, they whispered.
And at night under the yellow light,
while the parents played canasta,
moth wings bumped against the screens.
A child's swallowed screams went to the hearts of the pines
and were never let go.

The Pearl River is the dividing line,
winding through the red clay soil.
In the moonlight the river shines
like pearl.

Is that you?
Is it you?
Is it you, girl?
On the surface a water moccasin
carves its way home.
White as a madonna lily, a shadow
moves away under the dark green cloaks
of our forefathers. In daylight
a woman walks out the other side. Is it you?
The song curls back into her ear.
She pauses to bend over the new birth
of a sea horse from fern.
Young things are so fragile, she whispers,
and remembers the teacher who stroked the knuckle of her left
little finger. Only once did she become enraged
and break the scissors against the desk.

But fingers . . .
I've said what I could say
about them.

Three

Ashes

for Richard McCarthy, 1908–95

He was my landlord and my friend.
He pruned each camellia and the lemon tree
by hand, not too neat, *windswept*, he said.

It wasn't much of a hole in the earth.
It looked like someone had lifted out a plug
to set a fence post, maybe.
About the size of a coffee canister.
And the box, dark brown cardboard, was no fancy urn.
The lid stood open. The remains in a plastic bag
sealed with a tie, like a healthy grain.
A little puff of air blew some ashes up
just as the gardener—for so he seemed
in his work clothes and boots—unloosed the tie
and prepared to commend the spirit to the earth
under a red rose bush. Some settled on my lips,
I swear. They tasted salt, a pleasure
primitive and a bit perverse, like the taste of sperm or cunt.
When I spoke the words, *the Lord is my shepherd*, another voice
ghosted mine, barely audible, always a fraction behind.

These are the body of him
who lay zipped in hospital plastic
waiting on a gurney to be shipped
on the last passage. This is the cracked chest
where they tried to beat his heart back from death.
This is the squeezed oh of the mouth
where they inserted the tube to force his breath.
This is the dust that lighted on my lips.
This is the flesh I have tasted.

All of him fit in the box, the whole box of them
fit into the plug in the earth.
Then the gardener came again. With rake,
he covered the place with cedar chips.
The administrator—for so she seemed, detached
in her straight black dress—placed a tiny plaque
on a two-inch stem in the earth, blank,
soon to be engraved. We took her word. The markers
might have named the roses but they named the flesh
by which the roses were fed.

In the car I mopped my lips with moist tissue paper.
But the taste lives—that powerful—
so does the vision of the flesh unzipped.
They had not expected visitors
or they would have made him *more presentable,*
the man in white coat gave me a moment alone
with the body, and closed the door.
I'd never noticed his eyelashes,
now asleep against his cheeks
in the youth of death.
Richard gathered me
so many bundles of sticks,
neatly tied and stowed, for kindling.

At Green Gulch

The sorrel raised his head toward me.
I think he thought I had an apple
in my pocket or a lump of sugar.
Scratching an ankle with a hoof,
snatching grass tufts, grinding
his blunt, stained teeth,
he sidled over to where I stood
on the other side of the barbed fence.
The dapple-gray worked his way over too.
I sunk down on my knees in the lush grass,
the roundness of their bodies above me.
Then the dapple wandered off.
The sorrel reached across the fence,
I could see the barbs press his throat,
and proffered his long nose.
The muzzle, chocolate, quivering
beneath my stroke, so unlike . . . so
like the forehead of my friend,
dead just hours ago.

Wild Artichokes

Out behind the county hospital in Martinez, California—
where brain-injured boys thrown from motorcycles
without helmets convalesce
along with the old woman who cannot remember,
abandoned in the hallway on her wheeled potty chair—

uncared for in their beds,
the unruly artichokes metamorphose,
touched by the stroke of seasons
and the bee's sucking lips.
Above dragon-toothed leaves,
tight green fists burst purple into heads,
nodding day by day toward the barbed fence.

Oranges on the tree grow past brilliant.
Walnuts blacken and crumble between the fingers.
The diabetic man who lost a leg
learns he'll lose the other foot.
And the artichokes take on the oat
glow of the semi-desert hills,
become long-stemmed scepters in the dry breezes.

Just now, with a precarious reach,
I become a thief,
snapping off a single stem of three
sun-gilt faces, each thorn-ringed—
stealing, perhaps, for the pure pleasure of the deed
(as we are born to do, according to the saint)
and because forgotten beauty blesses us
forgotten sick.

Transplant

Strong men in plaid shirts and jeans
come from the waving silver-sleeved ocean
dawn into the bacon coffee haven, their breaths
hovering at the door, called back
to the company of the fog. Inside,
they puff their chests like proud dogs
and greet one another
in the male way,

       while I
cross my legs, an unfamiliar
here with yesterday's newspaper,
hug my table and the wall, invisible
I hope, examining the knucklebones cupped around my mug
for warmth, remembering Sartre's description
of the haunted physician, examining mechanically
his own examining hands. I am old enough to be
the mother of the girl who saw,

               opaque,
  through an aureole of peachy flesh,
  shadow bones of these hands
  lit by a flashlight held
  flush against her palm in a canyon
  in New Mexico. Jeffrey—

  black swash of hair, curled lip,
  wanted to be a physicist—
  lit his bones too. Within the safety
  of the tent, they made their faces,
  plastic with youth, into masks, and laughed,

while the protectors played canasta
outside by the lamp, night laced
with the fingers of light, and kept
the secrets.

　　　　　These men seem to know
themselves, the waitress
with the unkind fate of fixture
doesn't have to ask their orders, regular
regulars, comfortable in their bodies,
raising their voices, as if sheer bravado could drown
the roar of that incessant other,
ocean they live beside, remembered
but not recollected, as one saint said
of the forgotten god.

　　　　　　Awakened
by that roar, I lay in bed, spellbound,
listening and watching the sky transform
itself, a thousand veils of orange, pink, blue
light. "It would be a good time
to die," the woman told the therapist,
describing the kinds of light at sunrise,
then apologized for saying
"nothing significant."

Getting up from the funky bed
in the Capitola Venetian Motel,
village of pastel pink,
blue, green stucco, where the pipes
knocked all night, I scuffed
alongside the leaden, liquid home
of the leviathan, hands in my pockets,
shoulders hunched, in the envelope of solitude.

I had been dreaming in Spanish.
Up ahead I saw the rueful figure
on the knock-kneed horse lashing at spray
as though it were a dragon. I am still asking
his sixteenth-century question: crazy or not?
Half the students say he's crazy;
half say he's following his dream.

                              The specialty
of the house is banana walnut French toast,
the waitress recites in her fixture tone of voice—
sweet French bread stuffed with banana, walnuts,
and cream cheese, sautéed golden brown,
served with hot apricot sauce—my ally
between two othernesses, ocean and men,
both strange. I decide to try it.

                    On the front page
    of the *Chronicle* it says the girl from Stockton
    rejected the heart of the young break-dancer who secretly
    loved her and, in some dreadful premonition,
    told his mother he wanted to leave the dying girl
    his heart, then died himself three days later
    from a brain clot. Some think, the paper says,
    it was from spinning on his head. Donna,
    who lived for three years with Felipe's heart
    in her chest, said she tried not to think of him
    because it was so sad, but sometimes his face
    would just appear. She was waiting for someone else's
    heart when she took a noontime nap
    and didn't wake up. She became a celebrity,

the paper reports, eating jelly beans
with the president. Even before she died,
movie producers were vying for the rights.

Those who knew her say she was cheerful
and had wisdom beyond her age.

Jeffrey

> *became a physicist.*
> *That same camping trip he and I,*
> *larger than life, strode*
> *down the side of a volcano,*
> *each giant step sinking to the ankle*
> *in cinder.*

> Red Rover, Red Rover,
> come over, come over.

> *He teaches at the state university*
> *in Lafayette, Louisiana; and I*
> *deal in questions:*

> Who is the sorcerer?
> Do good intentions make a good man?

seminal questions of the Western world.

> Did Jeffrey offer me his heart?

From the slate

gray beach, a thousand seagulls lift at once
into the sky, I'll call them souls,
or holy ghosts, rising to the next
level of being,
like the thousand grooms and brides
married yesterday in Central Park
en masse by some maharishi.

Is there anyone for whom
　　you would give a leg or arm?

Half the students say
they would give their lives for a friend.
What naïveté, I say to myself.

Which would you say comes first,
　　self-love or love of a friend?

　　　　　　　　　　　　　That summer
I didn't give Jeffrey's heart a thought.
On an impulse I started up the canyon wall,
like a spider monkey, clutching
bits of brush for support.
I looked down. My stomach lurched
into my throat. Among tiny landslides
I inched my way back to the ground still innocent
of the complexities of fear.

　　　　　　　　　　Donna and Felipe
are the age my hands were back then,
too young for the knowledge of death. The saga of
Donna and Felipe, written by the quixotic
man upstairs. I'll see it
on the late late movie, I'll see her
eating jelly beans, I'll see him
spinning on his head.

　　Why does the knight let his horse
　　　　lead the way?
　　Why couldn't she accept his heart
　　　　and live?

While He Sleeps: A Meditation

His hand lies open on my chest,
my hand on his—bare facts
in the stark night,

the moment of hands and skin
given as the four o'clock rain is,
as rain gives texture to the darkness.

The moment flows back, then,
into history, where it always lives,
a continent we lug behind us
and, though we may forget, can never shed;
lodestar directing us from the rear.

Offer up a nod of the head or an unspoken prayer
even if a Giver doesn't see or hear.

On the sixth-month review Dianne was given
five new tumors in her abdomen. Bare facts.
If there is something you have longed to do,
do it, the surgeon is reported to have said.
Don't waste time on experimental cures.

Bare facts given by an unhearing
blindness in an act called grace—pure gift,
unearned, not merited, simply given

as the lightning is, just now,
as lightning electrifies the other world.

Aquarium

These tanks drain our human centers,
glowing, while our many bodies
fumble through the dark corridors,
feeling one another's heat,

drawn along by iridescent tentacles—unearthly
orange and pink—anemones
in their slow lives among reefs and fleshy seaweed.
Moray eels, the small-eyed sea salamander, snakes
like hung question marks.
Tank after tank we bear hypnotic witness
to the opening and closing of mouths,
the pulsing of gills. The giant sea bass,
manatees—the gentle sea cows—
piranha, blue angels,
and many others who will swim
nameless in memory
long after our leaving.

In this reverse of worlds, only we human beings
would wonder if they in the lit world wonder
about us, passing in our darkened channels.

Do we matter?

His hand reaches for mine, lest we lose ourselves,

and we who entered strangers come out
anemic by their indelible colors
and even more estranged.

The Yellow Stone

Like a nugget of gold underwater, the stone
glowed in the edge of the Yellowstone
River we had followed all day.
I thought it meant we
had been given a talisman,
and I reached into the mountain cold
and lifted it up, dripping
with the light death casts,
coming as it sometimes
does as love
in the last brightness.

                  We walked on the curve
of some other world, where droll
personalities of the under earth burped
and steamed at various intervals
in varying degrees of heat
from the terra firma. Smokey Joe,
Sleepy, Little Rainbow, Faithful Jr.—
we called them by name. And we
held hands.

        His is the hand
which has a stub for the left
thumb. He forced it in
my mouth, slipping it along
the teeth at the line of the
gum, that inner terrain
of privacy. He pushed it up
behind my lip and deep into the jaw
and down under the tongue. It was

a kind of death and a kind
of love.

      In that summer before
Yellowstone burned, a moose
came up to the car, clown-like,
balancing his heavy headdress, his lowers
hanging loose, as though he were
about to talk. I thought it meant
the one my love had called
our *us-being* had been sent another
guardian angel.

      Our love-being
had first appeared to him in a dream
of a baby girl circled all round
with brightness. She had appeared
again like a miracle
as a wide-eyed doll child
madonna dressed in a full white
dress in a small stone chapel
where we lit a single candle
for her care.

      We left Yellowstone
through the Grand Tetons. Breasts, he said,
and we headed up to find some place to eat
with a view. Finding nothing, we drove on
and on to Idaho, arriving after everything
had closed to some stinking fleabag
by the side of the road, too tired to go on,
starved.

      It must have been the next day
following the Snake that she
dried up, when we rolled newspaper

in the car windows to protect ourselves
from the heat and at night
sped alongside the searching
eye of the train. We weren't able
to stop then for anything. We had
to get to the end.

              We stopped
just this side of the Pacific
Ocean. Our last passion a killing
brightness. We had to veil
our eyes. Then he went off
the other side. And I stayed
holding the yellow stone
and the burnt shard of the yearling
babe, like the petrified tip
of his thumb with the bit
of unearthly black nail
which he kept on his desk
stuck in a piece of cork
by the pin they had used to graft it
back on, but the graft didn't take—
a relic of him—
even this I adored.

Visitation

Lying full-length in a porcelain
bathtub in Billings, Montana, lit shadows
of amoeboid forms feeling their way
across my breasts, the day
replaying its life as though
near death: the naked body
of my lover's daughter picking
her steps along the rim
of the lake, a goddess
of the heat and sage;
the sudden arising of swans
from the reeds; the ride back
in the sprung Capri, the goddess driving, her father
giving her first instruction
over the open range, recoiling barbed wire
cattle gates, grasshoppers
like popped corn flying
at me in the backseat, trying to speak wisely
to myself about jealousy: it is
an unbecoming emotion; wishing he
would turn his head and, if not speak,
smile or reach back a hand; speaking to myself
untenderly about anger, hate, and smallness
of heart; wishing his tight dark
body would come in to me as I bathed,
as the dust was releasing its claim
upon my skin—

as though a dark thought flew
out of my mind, I was visited by the bat,

the pounding of its wings magnified
a hundred times in my small white room,
around and around, dipping
toward the tub—I could just hear
the high-pitched sonar voice—a creature
as frightened as I was, I realize now,
but then I could only fear, shrinking back, back
into the porcelain, my nakedness
terrifying.

I would like to tell you the story ended like this:
that I took the mossy creature pulsing on the sill
into my hand, stroked the wrinkled forehead and listened
for his singing, or that I
gathered with him and also flew
through the open window, or, at the very least,
that I turned out the light and let him
find his own way back into the night, or,
as a last resort, that I got a broom and swept
the little fellow out the way I used to do
when, as a child, I felt it
a marvelous thing to have
a bat fly into the room.

But these are not the ways. No.
I gulped half-cries. I shrunk
back further into the tub
and remembered stories
of rabid bats, those that exhibit
unusual behavior, entering a window
of your home, for instance,
how the saliva could fall
into an open wound. I bolted
when I got the nerve, naked
through the bathroom door,
slammed it shut, and shrieked, shrieked.

They came running, goddess and lover.
She popped her head in
to see it. He got the broom. I repeated
stories of rabid bats. Before long
he emerged, broom in hand, carrying the bat—
he said he had to hit it hard—alien
flaccid on the straws, smaller than you'd think, the nearly
human face. He placed it on the upstairs porch
outside our bedroom. I went back
several times—it had not moved—baby
left to the mercies of night.

Our lovemaking was ecstatic—
I cried out wishing she would hear—and close
to brutal. In sleep I dreamed she too
was in our bed. He rode her as he had ridden me.
She turned, then, and the woman and I kissed.
I thought the bat
had regained
the pulse, had pulled
the small body back together
and winged forward
into the bare silver
dawn.

Four

The Sycamores

I looked up and saw a young sycamore
with fresh spring leaves and burrs of the old season.
When I was young on Sycamore Street,
my funny cream-colored dog, a foundling,
died in the dust at the edge of the front porch
of poisoning. Another time,
my mother began to wail
sitting at the dining room table.
One of God's frightened children,
I stood behind and held her,
not knowing what else to do.
She taught me to touch the cool new skin
beneath the shedding strips of bark on those old trees
with canopies that more than crossed the street . . .
as I did the night of the day the funny dog died,
standing in my silk organza, off-the-shoulder
dress, cheek pressed against the smooth silver,
looking up into the lamp-lit heart,
after John brought me home from the senior prom.

Breech

Because she breeched, her mother
doubted her. She came out
into thick air, that man's hands, her mother's fear.
For a long time she crawled rear first,
reaching a hand in the direction she was coming from . . .
What was I reaching for? seeing ahead
with those two shy eyes—waste and sex.
When she turned around, she saw

despair. She stood up
with the aid of a chair.
And then I saw the sea, what a clumsy gait
as she ran across the beach
to that light and entered *oh joy*
the lip of the sea.

A dream is a real thing.
Fear is the mother of fiction.
A hole is the author of shame.

If she could begin again, head first . . .
If he had not gripped me with his forceps . . .
If the tendon of her neck had not been torn . . .

If mother and daughter   *mirror . . . mirror*
could play the game over again:
Nod your little head left . . .
Nod your little head right . . .
Now forward . . . Now back . . .
Now roll it all the way around . . . roll it all around . . .

If they could begin again.
If I could look with eyes that love her
into the eyes of my mother, blue
with the skinny veins of . . . what?
Her mother wouldn't say, she would say
she was happy
despite long spells of . . . what?

I have a little shadow that goes in
and out . . .

Sunday morning . . .
over the telephone her mother speaks
of tomatoes, sweet peas,
the cardinal nesting in the fig tree,
the squirrel the destroyer.
The daughter at home in California
has a headache, bulbous as the eggplant swelling
on her mother's branch in Gretna, Louisiana.
Her mother is rolling up her pant legs
and wading once again into the sea of dew.
Winken, Blinken, and Nod sailed out . . .
She holds the purple fruit
in her hands. Perfect . . . perfect,
she coos. *Not me.*

Together they turn and see the dragonfly
hovering in a stroke of sunlight.
Each reticulated eye contains a world.
By day they are brave.
By night they cling.

At the Gulf

It was winter. The transparent swells
broke into foam along the edge. Light
bounced from beach back to steely sky.
The sun looked like it had had a hard night.
Wind-bitten, we with narrowed eyes, squinted
at them standing in air above our heads.
Black, gray, or white, every feather in
its place, the orange beak, the keen eye.
When we tossed up a pellet of the old dog's
food, they constellated around it, a perfect
winged design, a moment outside time,
until we tossed another, and they soared
to form a perfect other followed by
another. Oh sound of the sea,
voice, speak, out of the wind-thrown,
up from the burnt and water-rent ashes
of her. Tell me how we got from there
to this bodily nowhere, this
unrelenting flux, her liquid tomb,
their constellations perfect in time
locked in my mind, and you Mother and I
tossing the old dog's food to the winter sky.

Luminaria

The bougainvillea lets go a few
papery lanterns, luminaria of day
gracing the hard earth of autumn

.

Filaments of hair
torn by a mother's hand from a daughter's head

time slows nearly to a stop

she watches them settle through the surface
to the bottom of the tub

the worst child

.

Fish mouth opening
closing

giant sea bass behind glass
awesome dirigible

like the school principal

when I raise my hand, I mean
absolute silence

.

Men have the luxury of breasts
they can suckle, women have
a poor second in the male chest

his nickel nipple
a small comfort

.

Her blood coming down irregularly now
purple-black
clots

daughter without daughter

.

At night she goes into the tunnel
the others pressing sticky palms against her back
high on fear, they strain to see the old woman
who lives in there with the dog that looks like Ali Baba
her grandmother's spaniel who never learned to stay home
sailed away on an aircraft carrier with some sailors
who took him for a stray and made him their mascot
the old woman sends the dog out to do her work
drag one of them into the labyrinth that opens in the dark
from a child's second-story bedroom
and floats by day invisible
in the chinaberry limbs outside the window
when the little friends catch a glimpse
they turn and run, shrieking, shoving
she, the first, is the last
treading against the wall of backs
this happens again and again

.

In the change of life
she knows the mother's curse

.

Sometimes taking giant steps
sometimes walking on her toes

she avoids cracks in the sidewalk

.

The trigonometry teacher
does a hula in the middle of the street
for her

she speeds up the car
gives him a little scare

the best student

.

She hears the voice
there is no dream beyond this one

seeds of loveliness past their prime
fallen in the garden

.

He practices meditation
is initiated, guards the body
of the master, helps him dress
silently in street clothes or in robes

he hates
his mother, but instead
hates her

.

His father

.

She leaves school before noon and walks home alone
It's not fair she says to herself over and over
avoiding the cracks, the snakes in the grass

The teacher said I ran, I didn't run
I walked fast

her mother believes her
it would have been easier had she been
all bad

.

At first he used to say *I love you*
but became more like her mother

.

She dreams a mosquito hawk
bites her on top of the head
she swats it, it falls
she kneels down and sees its golden wings
my mother she says

he says *it is a good dream*

.

She offers him her breasts

.

Her mother wanted bougainvillea in the garden
but in her part of the country it freezes

.

She once fell in love with a Father
God loves you he used to tell her
the shape of his face reminded her
of her father's brother
he was the only lover approved by her mother
around him she became giddy as a girl

.

A mother's dream
planted in a daughter's garden
where it doesn't freeze

.

No matter
how faithfully he practices

.

Call them brave
practicing *perfection*

not *without mistake*
but *the thorough making of something*
the way her mother
shapes clay on the wheel
laying hands on
living with

a friend who died too young
who may have been a saint
used to say

.

bougainvillea
last lights of the dry season
flashing on earth
before the rain
autumn lengthening into winter
the blossoms
fragile paper lanterns, luminaria
turn brown and melt.

The Lawn Man

Nothing is to be negotiated
with the lawn man.
Protected in his helmet of noise,
he hears no complaints,
looks neither left nor right.
Just mows down
whatever stands in his way
and leaves the bill.

◆

Nothing roars like New Orleans thunder.
Chez Madeleine. Late August. No rain.
Just the heated conversation
of the heavens. And one,

two, three, four, five, six, now seven
sparrows, vying for crumbs
beneath the table. *Not one of these
is forgotten*, thunder the heavens with a jagged
exclamation point. *How much more
does your father care for you!*

And it *is* true: these sparrows
have their crumbs.

◆

This is the story of the small artists
of the world:

a sculpture in the garden,
terra-cotta clay, a totem,

each segment separately crafted,
fired in the kiln,
brought out whole with luck,
stacked one upon another on a pole,
each inspired by a certain spirit—
sparrow, leaf, furrowed brow, shadow—
and by no one's vision but hers.

Through thunder, rain, humidity, heat,
the cool autumns, for thirty years
my mother's totem has watched over
this small fenced province
among the adjoining provinces
where she has passed.

Now, cracked at the base
by an indifferent lawn man
it is beginning to fall.
At least the grass gets cut,
my father says, too gray to quibble.
Only the daughter, childless,
visiting from the West Coast,
cares enough to attempt repairs.

The Swamp Walk

Almost a creature itself, wooden planks
on pilings, it walks across the swamp
at Barataria State Park. Below,
the bayou quivers with the barest motion
of alligator, turtle, gar, the spider bugs
that light on water. The resonance
of footfalls on weathered wood.
It is Sunday, and the seniors are out
on their weekend excursion.
They are comparing their ages. And
my father is there with his cane, in the days
before the walker. He is preparing to
step forward and announce that he is the oldest,
ninety-three. Just as he does—and it seems
I've known it all along—he loses his balance.
I lunge into the dream. Grab hold of him,
a foot, a leg, already impossibly gone
with the sunlight through a crack into the bayou.

Perfect Tree

March 6

All your smallest branches were laced
with frost, in the moonlight,
spun, an intricate net,
strong enough to catch even gods
if they should fall.

March 7

An owl appeared, shadow,
on your lowest branch and turned his head around
to the right and then the left. He left to deal death,
toward the ground, talons first. They who were
turned prey, not in my range of sight.

March 8

A more frequent visitor, and by day,
the blue tit, who swipes his little beak along a branch,
side to side, as a knife sharpener slides the flint
along a blade one side then the other.
Sometimes they are two in your limbs,
nodding their blue-black caps, extending
their lemony yellow breasts to the sun.

March 9

In rain, too, you glisten, but are not spun
by light; and in wind you are so closely knit

that all your branches tremble as a whole
down to the smallest twig.

March 10

You were grown straight by the wheel
of nature; though still in your youth, with a fine
knowing of how to present yourself to the world.
Not an inch of pride. Hiding out from nothing. Simply beautiful.

March 11

When the pruners came to shape the olive trees,
they also took their shears to the other trees standing around
as young trees do, but they left you alone.

March 12

I have a feeling you were grown for a special reason,
planted outside the window by a person
I do not know, maybe in memory of a sister,
or a favorite pet, but I can guess that she who planted you
was at a loss, and did not want to be alone, and needed a friend,
as I am and do not and need you.
How graciously you take the role.

March 13

Spinoza wrote, *Only those who are very free
are very grateful to one another. . . .*
You have freely given your presence to me;
and I have given to you my gaze
all winter long. Even in the night
you glow into the room.

March 14

Goodbye, silver sister of my young mother, before I knew her.

(*Greve in Chianti*)

in
gratitude

From the Foot of Fourth Street

Louisville, Kentucky

for James Wright

So this is the Ohio,
river that you longed for,
some holiness you said *was dying*,
border of three states.
From this Kentucky bank,
it looks wide,
wide as the Mississippi,
and it doesn't look like it's dying.
It looks alive
in a lazy Southern way.
Guided by the tug *Miss Nari*,
the block-long *River Explorer*
is edging toward the dock.
Tourists on top wave at folks
on the deck of Joe's Crab Shack.
(Joe knows everything there is to know
about crabs.) One or two wave back.
Moored for her noon nap, *Belle*
the riverboat daydreams in the sun,
her flags fluttering up.
Well-designed riverside:
waterfront parks and strategic bronze plaques
placed to tell history stage by stage.
From this spot Lewis and Clark
began their expedition.
And next we learn that York
was with them, slave,

celebrated now, the first black man
to make it coast to coast.
And here where the bank is high,
York is standing, more than life-sized,
looking over the Ohio.
Below him, three men and a woman bow
forehead to the ground in homage,
murmuring to themselves,
Here is the lotus land,
this very body the Buddha.
No riffraff river. River
sparkling clean. Dimpled,
not laughing, smiling
river in the hot summer breeze.
But when I look in, river that reveals
opaque green density.
Nothing of the underneath
you saw as a child from its banks
in Martin's Ferry, your Ohio,
grappling hooks dragging the bottom
for the bodies of children.
And later, as the sun goes down
orange on your river, at the *Fish Bar*
in the Galt Hotel—an aquarium
swimming beneath my elbows—
I order a Jack Daniel's,
my own sort of homage to the South,
take slow sips gazing out . . . *river on earth,*
stay with me a little longer . . .
as though memorizing memory.

I thank the editors of the following journals in which these poems first appeared:

The Hudson Review: "The Pearl River"

Literary Imagination (Oxford University Press): "The Sycamores," vol. 11, no. 3 (2009), 328, first published online July 24, 2009; "From the Foot of Fourth Street, Louisville, Kentucky," vol. 12, no. 1 (2010), 52–53, first published online July 24, 2009; "The Pianist," "Breech," and "The Lawn Man," vol. 14, no. 1 (2011), 68–69, 70–71, and 72–73, respectively, first published online November 17, 2011.

Naugatuck River Review: "Wild Artichokes"

North American Review: "Ashes"

Northeast Corridor: "Fencing"

Ploughshares: "Visitation"

Quarterly Review of Literature: "Transplant" and "The Yellow Stone," by permission of Quarterly Review of Literature (QRL) Archives; 1943–2000, Manuscripts Division, Department of Rare Books and Special Collections, Princeton University Library

The Southern Review: "Listening to a Shell"

TriQuarterly: "Luminaria" and "Perfect Tree"

Turning Wheel: "Painting a Still Life with My Mother"

Zebra: "The Bridge"

◆

I am grateful to the Faculty Development Fund of Saint Mary's College of California for support in completing this collection.

Gratitude also goes to the English Department of Tulane University for the invitation to spend a semester as Visiting Poet in Residence in New Orleans, where some of these poems were written.

Also gratitude to the Squaw Valley Community of Writers, where others of these poems were written.

◆

My deepest thanks to

My parents—
my mother, for instilling the spirit of poetry in me from my earliest years;
my father, for being proud of me and believing in my poetic endeavor.
I wish that they were here now.

My brother, Chuck, and his wife, Dorothy.

My mentor, James Wright.

My teacher, Robert Kimball.

Richard McCarthy, who gave me a place to write.

My initial readers—Paul Breslin, who brought my poetry to the attention of Northwestern; Richard Wertime, who has believed in my work through thick and thin; and Richard Tillinghast, who suggested a reordering and a new title.

So many have helped me along the way—Peter Campion, Peter Cooley, Galway Kinnell, Robert Hass, Gerald Stern, Jean Valentine, Natasha Trethewey, Kay Murphy and members of the poetry group in New Orleans, Albione Becnel, Thomas Berglund, Gary Whitmer, Alice Jones, Alan Goldfarb, Ed Smallfield, Ann Barrows, Naomi Schwartz, Jack Marshall, Bill Hynes, members of the poetry group in Berkeley, including Peter Dale Scott, Chana Bloch, Diana O'Hehir, Sandra Gilbert, Dan Bellm, and especially Phyllis Stowell.

My thanks as well to colleagues at Saint Mary's College. I would like to mention in particular David Gentry-Akin, Penny Washbourn, and Stephen Woolpert.

Very special thanks to Parneshia Jones, for choosing this book for Northwestern University Press.

Dove and Snow, for their furry comfort.

Elizabeth Williamson and Alan Williamson for being there.